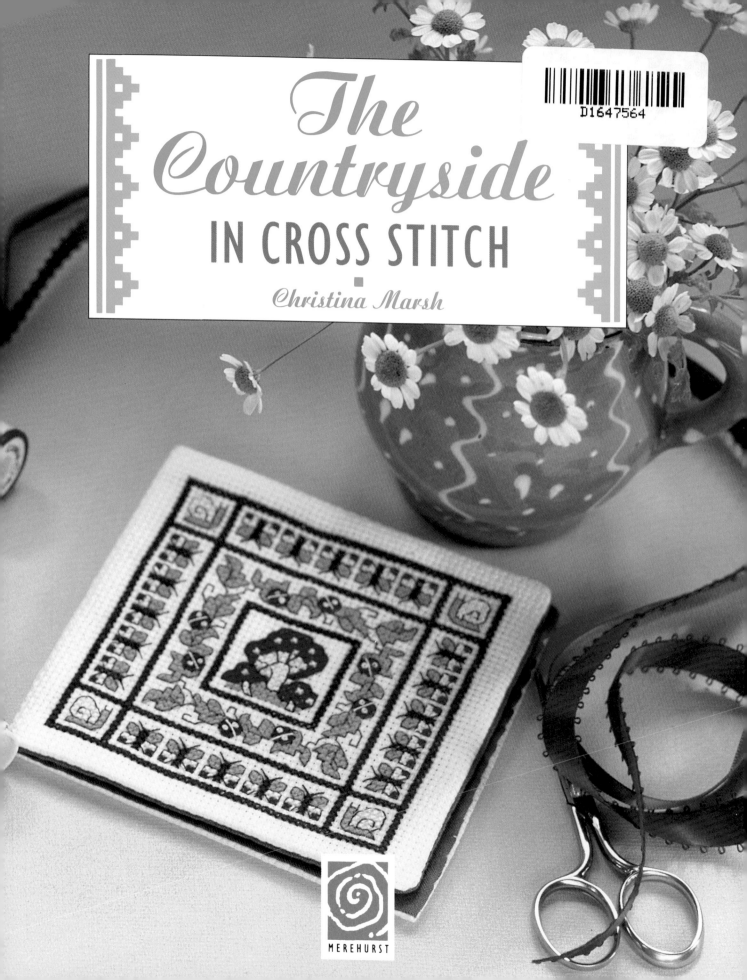

The Countryside
IN CROSS STITCH

Christina Marsh

MEREHURST

THE CHARTS

Some of the designs in this book are very detailed and due to inevitable space limitations, the charts may be shown on a comparatively small scale; in such cases, readers may find it helpful to have the particular chart with which they are currently working enlarged.

THREADS

The projects in this book were all stitched with Anchor stranded cotton embroidery threads. The keys given with each chart also list thread combinations for those who wish to use DMC or Madeira threads. It should be pointed out that the shades produced by different companies vary slightly, and it is not always possible to find identical colours in a different range.

Published in 1995 by Merehurst Limited
Ferry House, 51-57 Lacy Road, Putney, London SW15 1PR
Text, photography & illustrations © Copyright 1995 Merehurst Limited
ISBN 1 85391 451 7

A catalogue record for this book is available from the British Library.

Commissioning Editor: Cheryl Brown
Edited by Diana Lodge
Designed by Maggie Aldred
Photography by Marie-Louise Avery
Illustrations by John Hutchinson
Typesetting by Dacorum Type & Print, Hemel Hempstead
Colour separation by Fotographics Limited, UK – Hong Kong
Printed in Hong Kong by Wing King Tong

Merehurst is the leading publisher of craft books and has an excellent range of titles to suit all levels. Please send to the address above for our free catalogue, stating the title of this book.

CONTENTS

INTRODUCTION

The beauties of nature – the fragility of wild flowers, the small animals of the meadows, hedges and woodlands, the colours of butterflies – and the simple pleasures of country life, are here celebrated in a selection of cross stitch designs created to please city dwellers just as much as those who live in the country.

Cross stitch is one of the oldest and simplest of embroidery stitches, and well suited to this traditional theme. It is a wonderfully easy stitch to learn – some of the more straightforward designs in this book would prove ideal for children wanting to learn embroidery – but whether you are young or old, you do not require years of experience to produce attractive results. The more subtly shaded designs may seem daunting at first, but your skill will quickly improve with practice.

Each design is carefully charted and colour coded, and there are step-by-step instructions for making up the item shown in the accompanying photograph.

The Basic Skills section covers everything from preparing your fabric and stretching it in a hoop or frame, to the simple cross, half cross and back stitches used in these designs, and mounting your finished embroidery, ready for display.

Whether you are a newcomer to cross stitch or a skilled embroiderer, you will enjoy stitching these delightful designs, creating beautiful things for your family and friends, and for your own home.

BASIC SKILLS

BEFORE YOU BEGIN

PREPARING THE FABRIC
Even with an average amount of handling, many evenweave fabrics tend to fray at the edges, so it is a good idea to overcast the raw edges, using ordinary sewing thread, before you begin.

FABRIC
All projects in this book use Aida fabric, which is ideal both for beginners and more advanced stitchers as it has a surface of clearly designated squares. All Aida fabric has a count, which refers to the number of squares (each stitch covers one square) to one inch (2.5cm); the higher the count, the smaller the finished stitching. Projects in this book use 11-, 14- or 18-count Aida, popular and readily available sizes, in a wide variety of colours.

THE INSTRUCTIONS
Each project begins with a full list of the materials that you will require. The measurements given for the embroidery fabric include a minimum of 5cm (2in) all around to allow for stretching it in a frame and preparing the edges to prevent them from fraying.

Colour keys for stranded embroidery cottons – Anchor, DMC or Madeira – are given with each chart. It is assumed that you will need to buy one skein of each colour mentioned in a particular key, even though you may use less, but where two or more skeins are needed, this information is included in the main list of requirements.

Before you begin to embroider, always mark the centre of the design with two lines of basting stitches, one vertical and one horizontal, running from edge to edge of the fabric, as indicated by the arrows on the charts.

As you stitch, use the centre lines given on the chart and the basting threads on your fabric as reference points for counting the squares and threads to position your design accurately.

WORKING IN A HOOP

A hoop is the most popular frame for use with small areas of embroidery. It consists of two rings, one fitted inside the other; the outer ring usually has an adjustable screw attachment so that it can be tightened to hold the stretched fabric in place. Hoops are available in several sizes, ranging from 10cm (4in) in diameter to quilting hoops with a diameter of 38cm (15in). Hoops with table stands or floor stands attached are also available.

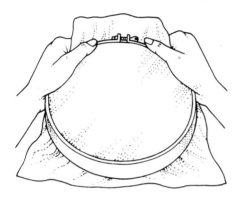

1 To stretch your fabric in a hoop, place the area to be embroidered over the inner ring and press the outer ring over it, with the tension screw released. Tissue paper can be placed between the outer ring and the embroidery, so that the hoop does not mark the fabric. Lay the tissue paper over the fabric when you set it in the hoop, then tear away the central embroidery area.

2 Smooth the fabric and, if necessary, straighten the grain before tightening the screw. The fabric should be evenly stretched.

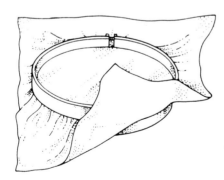

WORKING IN A RECTANGULAR FRAME

Rectangular frames are more suitable for larger pieces of embroidery. They consist of two rollers, with tapes attached, and two flat side pieces, which slot into the rollers and are held in place by pegs or screw attachments. Available in different sizes, either alone or with adjustable table or floor stands, frames are measured by the length of the roller tape, and range in size from 30cm (12in) to 68cm (27in).

As alternatives to a slate frame, canvas stretchers and the backs of old picture frames can be used. Provided there is sufficient extra fabric around the finished size of the embroidery, the edges can be turned under and simply attached with drawing pins (thumb tacks) or staples.

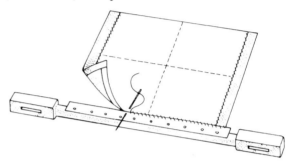

1 To stretch your fabric in a rectangular frame, cut out the fabric, allowing at least an extra 5cm (2in) all around the finished size of the embroidery. Baste a single 12mm (½in) turning on the top and bottom edges and oversew strong tape, 2.5cm (1in) wide, to the other two sides. Mark the centre line both ways with basting stitches. Working from the centre outward and using strong thread, oversew the top and bottom edges to the roller tapes. Fit the side pieces into the slots, and roll any extra fabric on one roller until the fabric is taut.

2 Insert the pegs or adjust the screw attachments to secure the frame. Thread a large-eyed needle (chenille needle) with strong thread or fine string and lace both edges, securing the ends around the intersections of the frame. Lace the webbing at 2.5cm (1in) intervals, stretching the fabric evenly.

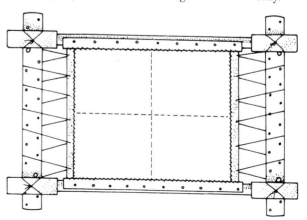

EXTENDING EMBROIDERY FABRIC

It is easy to extend a piece of embroidery fabric, such as a bookmark, to stretch it in a hoop.

● Fabric oddments of a similar weight can be used. Simply cut four pieces to size (in other words, to the measurement that will fit both the embroidery fabric and your hoop) and baste them to each side of the embroidery fabric before stretching it in the hoop in the usual way.

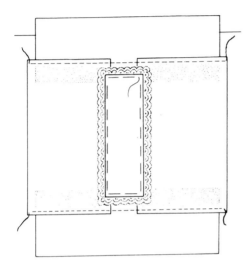

MOUNTING EMBROIDERY

The cardboard should be cut to the size of the finished embroidery, with an extra 6mm (¼in) added all round to allow for the recess in the frame.

LIGHTWEIGHT FABRICS

1 Place embroidery face down, with the cardboard centred on top, and basting and pencil lines matching. Begin by folding over the fabric at each corner and securing it with masking tape.

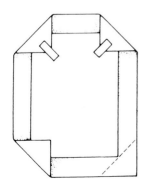 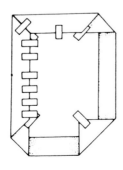

2 Working first on one side and then the other, fold over the fabric on all sides and secure it firmly with pieces of masking tape, placed about 2.5cm (1in) apart. Also neaten the mitred corners with masking tape, pulling the fabric tightly to give a firm, smooth finish.

HEAVIER FABRICS

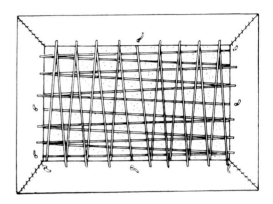

● Lay the embroidery face down, with the cardboard centred on top; fold over the edges of the fabric on opposite sides, making mitred folds at the corners, and lace across, using strong thread. Repeat on the other two sides. Finally, pull up the fabric firmly over the cardboard. Overstitch the mitred corners.

CROSS STITCH

For all cross stitch embroidery, the following two methods of working are used. In each case, neat rows of vertical stitches are produced on the back of the fabric.

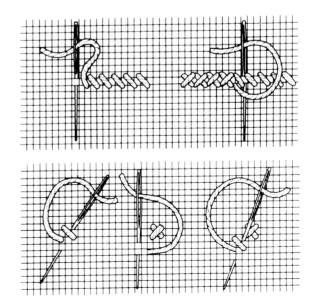

● When stitching large areas, work in horizontal rows. Working from right to left, complete the first row of evenly spaced diagonal stitches over the number of threads specified in the project instructions. Then, working from left to right, repeat the process. Continue in this way, making sure each stitch crosses in the same direction.

● When stitching diagonal lines, work downwards, completing each stitch before moving to the next. When starting a project always begin to embroider at the centre of the design and work outwards to ensure that the design will be placed centrally on the fabric.

BACKSTITCH

Backstitch is used in the projects to give emphasis to a particular foldline, an outline or a shadow. The stitches are worked over the same number of threads as the cross stitch, forming continuous straight or diagonal lines.

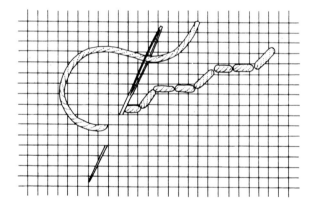

● Make the first stitch from left to right; pass the needle behind the fabric and bring it out one stitch length ahead to the left. Repeat and continue in this way along the line.

THREE-QUARTER CROSS STITCHES

Some fractional stitches are used on certain projects in this book; although they strike fear into the hearts of less experienced stitchers they are not difficult to master, and give a more natural line in certain instances. Should you find it difficult to pierce the centre of the Aida block, simply use a sharp needle to make a small hole in the centre first.

To work a three-quarter cross, bring the needle up at point A and down through the centre of the square at B. Later, the diagonal back stitch finishes the stitch. A chart square with two different symbols separated by a diagonal line requires two 'three-quarter' stitches. Backstitch will later finish the square.

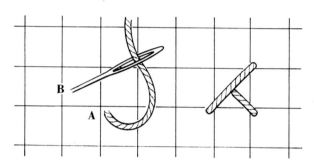

FRENCH KNOTS

This stitch is shown on some of the diagrams by a small dot. Where there are several french knots, the dots have been omitted to avoid confusion. Where this occurs you should refer to the instructions of the project and the colour photograph.

To work a french knot, bring your needle and cotton out slightly to the right of where you want your knot to be. Wind the thread once or twice around the needle, depending on how big you want your knot to be, and insert the needle to the left of the point where you brought it out.

Be careful not to pull too hard or the knot will disappear through the fabric. The instructions state the number of strands of cotton to be used for the french knots.

Hedgerow Sampler

The traditional sampler is given a new look with this charming combination of blue tits, butterflies and berries. If you don't want to make a sampler, either the butterflies or the birds could be repeated to make a border, perhaps for a towel or a tablecloth.

HEDGEROW SAMPLER

YOU WILL NEED

For the sampler, set in a frame with an aperture measuring 28.5cm × 24.5cm (11½in × 9½in):

46cm × 38cm, (18in × 15in) of ivory,
11-count Aida fabric
Stranded embroidery cotton in the colours given
in the panel
No24 tapestry needle
Picture frame, with a cut-out as specified above
Firm card, to fit the frame
Lightweight synthetic batting, the same
size as the card
Strong thread, for mounting
Glue stick
Four small black beads and a beading needle
(optional)

●

THE EMBROIDERY

Prepare the fabric as described on page 4; find the centre either by folding the fabric in half and then in half again, and lightly pressing the folded corner, or by marking the horizontal and vertical centre lines with basting stitches in a light-coloured thread. Mount the fabric in a frame (see page 5) and start the design from the centre.

Following the chart, complete all the cross stitching first, using two strands of thread in the needle. Finish with the backstitching, again using two strands of thread. Be careful not to take dark threads across the back of the work in such a way that they show through on the right side.

The birds' eyes, indicated by black dots on the chart, can either be made with a single french knot for each, stitched with two strands of black thread, or you can use a small black bead for each eye.

MOUNTING AND FRAMING

Remove the embroidery from the frame and wash if necessary, then press lightly on the wrong side, using a steam iron and taking extra care if you have used beads for the eyes. Spread glue evenly on one side of the mounting card, and lightly press the batting to the surface. Lace the embroidery over the padded surface (see page 6). Remove basting stitches, place the embroidery in the frame, and assemble the frame according to the manufacturer's instructions.

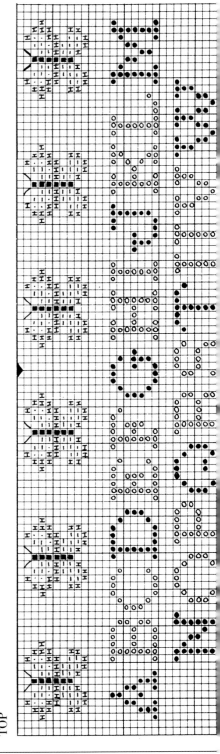

TOP

HEDGEROW SAMPLER ▲	ANCHOR	DMC	MADEIRA
H Blue	979	312	1005
− Light yellow green	278	472	1414
+ Medium yellow green	280	733	1609
V Medium green	267	580	1608
∧ Dark green	268	935	1504

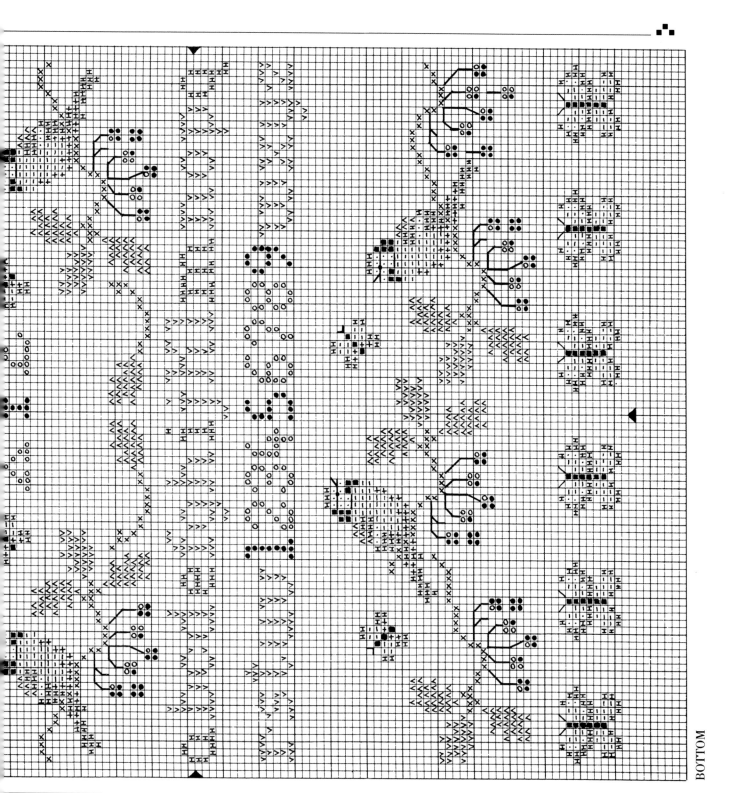

		ANCHOR	DMC	MADEIRA
•	White	1	Blanc	White
X	Brown	360	898	2006
■	Black	430	Black	Black
○	Bright red	19	817	212
●	Dark red	20	498	513

Note: bks the butterfly feelers, birds' eye lines and beaks in black, and the cherry stalks in dark green. Using two strands of thread in the needle, form each bird's eye with a french knot, unless using beads.

Country Village

Five pictures – a church, the traditional village inn, and three cottages – put them together and you have the essence of a typical small hamlet. Alternatively, any of these designs would make a charming card; the church would be ideal for a wedding, for example, or a little house could mark a housewarming.

COUNTRY VILLAGE

YOU WILL NEED

For either the *Church* or the *Inn*, each set in a
frame with a centre measuring
11.5cm × 7.5cm (4½in × 3in):

*25cm × 17.5cm (10in × 7in) of blue,
14-count Aida fabric
Stranded embroidery cotton in the colours given
in the appropriate panel
No26 tapestry needle
Picture frame, with a cut-out as specified above
Firm card, to fit the frame
Lightweight synthetic batting, the same size
as the card
Masking tape for mounting
Glue stick*

For each house/cottage picture, each set in a frame
with a centre measuring 7.5cm (3in) square:

*17.5cm (7in) square of blue, 14-count Aida fabric
Picture frame with a cut-out as specified above.
Stranded embroidery cotton, tapestry needles, firm
card, synthetic batting, masking tape and glue, as for
Church and Inn.*

*NOTE: if you are making all five pictures at the same
time, you will find that 46cm × 38cm (18in × 15in)
of Aida fabric will be sufficient. One skein of stranded
cotton in each of the colours listed on the charts will
be sufficient to complete all five designs; if you wish
to embroider a single design, buy only the colours
indicated on the relevant chart.*

•

THE EMBROIDERY

Prepare the edges of the fabric as described on page
4. If you are making all five designs, baste along the
lines separating the five pictures, ensuring that you
leave a margin of fabric around each picture area for
mounting (see below), but do not cut the fabric.
Baste horizontal and vertical centre lines across
each section to mark the centre of each picture area.
Mount the fabric in a frame (see page 5) and start
each design from the centre.

If you are stitching a single design, find the centre
either by folding the fabric in half and then in half
again, and lightly pressing the folded corner, or by
marking the horizontal and vertical centre lines with
basting stitches in a light-coloured thread. For

individual designs there is no need to mount the
fabric in a hoop or frame.

Following the chart(s), complete all the cross
stitching first, using two strands of thread in the
needle. Finish with the backstitching and the french
knots, again using two strands of thread.

MOUNTING AND FRAMING

Remove the finished embroidery from the frame and
wash if necessary, then press lightly on the wrong
side, using a steam iron. If you have stitched all
designs on the same piece of fabric, cut along the
dividing lines.

For each design, spread glue evenly on one side of
the mounting card, and lightly press the batting to
the surface. Tape the embroidery over the padded
surface (see page 6), using the basting stitches (if
any) to check that the embroidery is centred over
the card. Remove basting stitches, place the
mounted embroidery in the frame, and assemble the
frame according to the manufacturer's instructions.

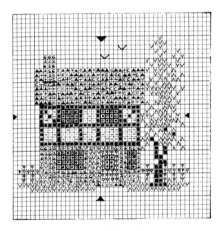

COUNTRY HOME ▲		ANCHOR	DMC	MADEIRA
•	White	1	Blanc	White
–	Light cream	386	746	101
I	Cream	885	3770	2001
?	Pale blue	130	799	1004
○	Medium blue	979	312	1005
●	Navy	127	939	1009
v	Light green	261	3363	1602
^	Medium green	262	3051	1603
2	Light brown	369	435	2010
6	Medium brown	370	433	2008
■	Dark brown	905	3781	2106
+	Light blue grey	848	927	1708
C	Light beige	373	3046	2103
▲	Dark beige	375	420	2105
	Pink*	48	818	502

*Note: bks the window frames in white, the birds in navy, and the
base of the chimney in dark brown. Work the flowers over the door
and along the flower bed in french knots, using *pink (used for bks
only) and pale blue.*

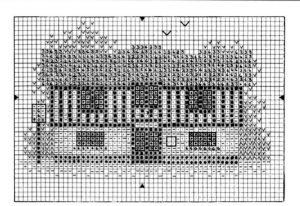

INN ▲		ANCHOR	DMC	MADEIRA
•	White	1	Blanc	White
−	Light cream	386	746	101
I	Cream	885	3770	2001
?	Pale blue	130	799	1004
○	Medium blue	979	312	1005
●	Navy	127	939	1009
v	Light green	261	3363	1602
∧	Medium green	262	3051	1603
2	Light brown	369	435	2010
6	Medium brown	370	433	2008
■	Dark brown	905	3781	2106
3	Dark warm brown	358	437	1910

Note: bks the window frames in white, the birds in navy, and the sign post and menu to the right of the door in dark brown. Fill window box with french knots in light green and pale blue.

THE GABLES ▲		ANCHOR	DMC	MADEIRA
•	White	1	Blanc	White
−	Light cream	386	746	101
○	Medium blue	979	312	1005
●	Navy	127	939	1009
v	Light green	261	3363	1602
∧	Medium green	262	3051	1603
6	Medium brown	370	433	2008
■	Dark brown	905	3781	2106
+	Light blue grey	848	927	1708
L	Very light beige	372	739	1909
Ɛ	Medium beige	374	3045	2104
▲	Dark beige	375	420	2105
	Pink*	48	818	502

Note: bks the window frames in white, the birds in navy, and the base of the chimney and lines of the wall in dark brown. Work the flowers on the bush and in the flower bed in french knots, using pink (used for bks only) and pale blue.*

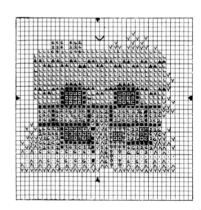

THATCHED COTTAGE ▲		ANCHOR	DMC	MADEIRA
•	White	1	Blanc	White
?	Pale blue	130	799	1004
○	Medium blue	979	312	1005
●	Navy	127	939	1009
v	Light green	261	3363	1602
∧	Medium green	262	3051	1603
6	Medium brown	370	433	2008
■	Dark brown	905	3781	2106
L	Very light beige	372	739	1909
	Pink*	48	818	502

Note: bks the window frames in white and the bird in navy. Work the flowers over the door and along the fence in french knots, using pink (used for bks only) and pale blue.*

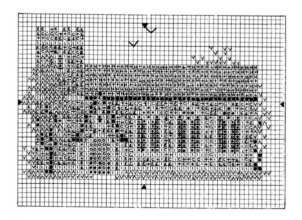

CHURCH ▲		ANCHOR	DMC	MADEIRA
I	Cream	885	3770	2001
○	Medium blue	979	312	1005
●	Navy	127	939	1009
v	Light green	261	3363	1602
∧	Medium green	262	3051	1603
■	Dark brown	905	3781	2106
+	Light blue grey	848	927	1708
H	Medium blue grey	920	932	710
C	Light beige	373	3046	2103
Ɛ	Medium beige	374	3045	2104

Note: bks the window frames in cream, and the birds in navy.

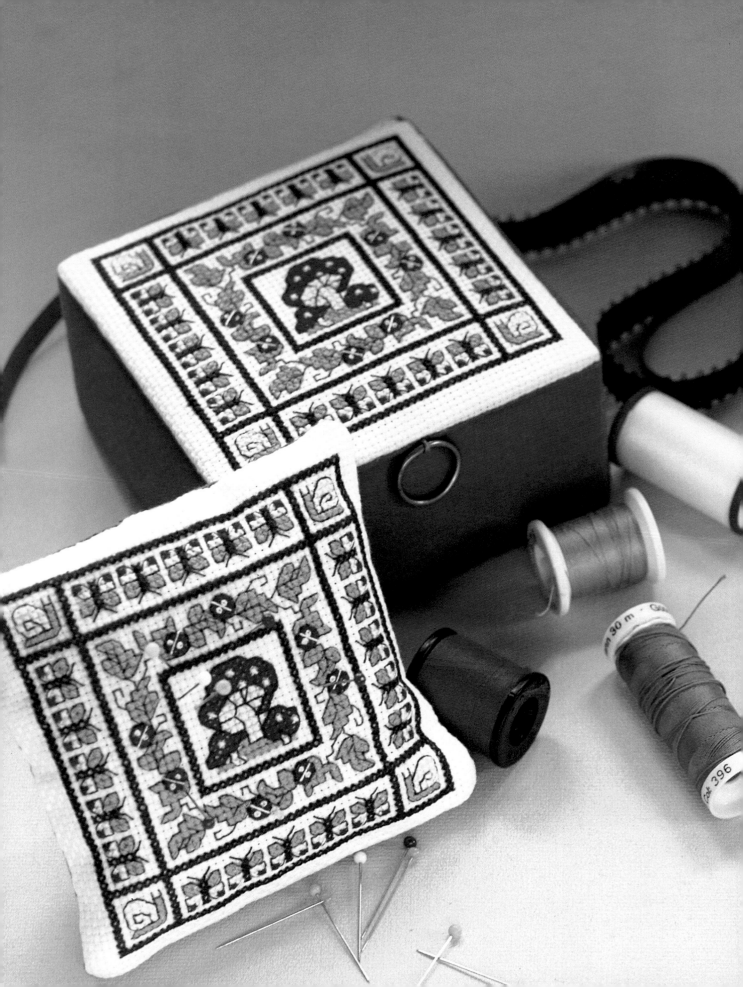

Woodland Magic

Ladybirds, butterflies, snails and toadstools create a simple square design that can be adapted to a multitude of uses. A pin cushion, needlecase and box are shown here, but the design would also make a charming birthday card, while either the outer or inner border, or both, could be used for a picture frame.

WOODLAND MAGIC

For the pin cushion, measuring
10cm (4in) square:

20cm (8in) square of white, 14-count Aida fabric
12.5cm (5in) square of green cotton fabric,
for backing
Stranded embroidery cotton in the colours
given in the panel
No26 tapestry needle
Wool, kapok or polyester filling

For the needlecase, measuring
10cm (4in) square:

30cm × 20cm (12 × 8in) of white,
14-count Aida fabric
24cm × 12.5cm (9½ × 5in) of green backing fabric
20cm × 10cm (8in × 4in) of green felt
Stranded embroidery cotton in the colours given
in the panel
No26 tapestry needle

For the box, 5cm (2in) deep, with a top measuring
10cm (4in) square:

20cm (8in) square of white, 14-count Aida fabric
Stranded embroidery cotton in the colours given
in the panel
No26 tapestry needle
Seven pieces of green cotton fabric,
each 12.5cm (5in) square
Stiff card (medium thickness) – four pieces
5cm × 10cm (2in × 4in),
and four pieces 10cm (4in) square
Lightweight polyester batting –
four pieces 5cm × 10cm (2in × 4in),
and one piece 10cm (4in) square
25cm (10in) of thin white cord
Small brass curtain ring
Glue stick
Masking tape
Strong thread for lacing

•

THE EMBROIDERY

For either the pin cushion or the box, start by preparing the fabric as described on page 4; find the centre either by folding the fabric in half and then in half again, and lightly pressing the folded corner, or by marking the horizontal and vertical centre lines with basting stitches in a light-coloured thread. Mount the fabric in a hoop (see page 4) and start the design from the centre.

If you are making the needlecase, start by folding the fabric in half and half again, to find the centre and then baste a rectangle measuring 21.5cm × 10cm (8½in × 4in) around the centre of the fabric. On the right-hand half of the rectangle (the front of the needlecase) mark the centre of this half only with horizontal and vertical lines of basting stitches in a light coloured thread. This centre is the centre of the design.

Following the chart and working from the centre outwards, complete all the cross stitching first, using two strands of thread in the needle. Finish with the backstitching, again using two strands of thread. Remove the finished embroidery from the hoop and wash if necessary, then press lightly on the wrong side, using a steam iron.

PIN CUSHION

Keeping the design centred, trim the Aida to measure 12.5cm (5in) square. Remove basting stitches. Place the embroidery and backing fabric right sides together and stitch around the sides, taking a 12mm (½in) seam allowance and leaving a small gap in one side for the filling. Trim across the seam allowance at the corners; turn the pin cushion right side out and fill tightly. Slipstitch across the opening.

NEEDLECASE

Trim the embroidery fabric, leaving a 12mm (½in) seam allowance around the basted rectangle. Remove basting stitches. Place the embroidery and backing fabric with right sides together and stitch around the edge, taking a 12mm (½in) seam allowance and leaving a small gap, for turning, on the lower edge at the blank half of the fabric. Trim across the seam allowance at the corners; turn the fabric right side out and slipstitch the gap. Using pinking shears, trim the felt to fit inside the needlecase, then attach it inside the centre fold, using small running stitches.

BOX

To prepare the side sections, first glue a piece of batting to one side of the each of the four 5cm × 10cm (2in × 4in) pieces of card. For each side, take a piece of green fabric and lay a card piece, padded side down, on the wrong side of the fabric, with an allowance of 12mm (½in) of fabric showing at each side, and a scant 15mm (⅝in) showing at the bottom edge. Fold in the sides and tape them, as shown. Bring the lower edge of the fabric up over the card; turn under a 12mm (½in) allowance along the top edge and bring it down to cover the lower raw edge of fabric. Stitch along the lower edge, so that the stitching line is just slightly to the back of the card, not along the bottom. Oversewing the edges with neat stitches, join the four sides of the box together to make a square, with the stitched lower edges facing inwards.

Take three square sections (base and inside lid) and cover one side of each with a piece of fabric: mitre the corners and fold in the sides, holding them with tape (see page 6). With the fabric outside, gently push one base section into the prepared side piece and neatly oversew the bottom edge on all sides. Turn the box over and neatly stitch white cord along the top edge of one side (now the back edge), allowing the ends to run down the inside corners and onto the base. Push the second base piece,

fabric side up, into the box, covering the cord ends and the back of the first base section.

Keeping the design centred, trim the embroidery to measure 12.5cm (5in) square, and remove basting stitches. Glue batting to one side of the remaining uncovered piece of card, and lace the work over the padded card (see page 6). Place the two lid sections with wrong sides together and neatly oversew the edges. Stitch the lid to the cord at the back of the box, and stitch the brass ring to the front centre edge of the lid.

WOODLAND MAGIC ▼		ANCHOR	DMC	MADEIRA
◯	Leaf green	226	702	1306
●	Brown	352	300	2304
·	Lemon	292	746	101
X	Red	47	304	511
	Dark green*	228	700	1304

Note: bks butterfly feelers, snail shells and toadstools in brown, butterfly wings, ladybirds, leaves and snail bodies in dark green* (used for bks only), and the central line down the ladybirds in lemon. Make one french knot on each side of the central line down the ladybirds, using two strands of lemon.

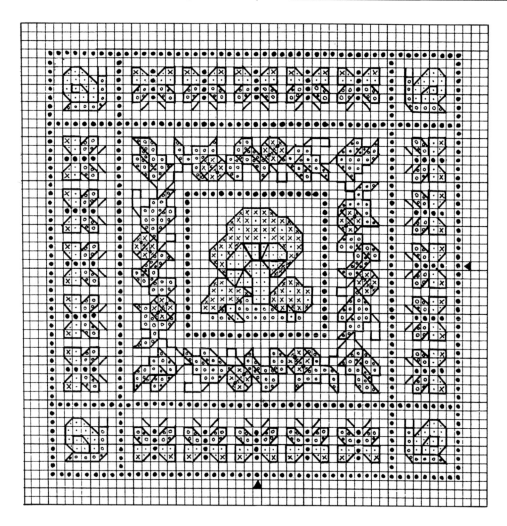

Butterflies

The ecological way to mount and frame butterflies is demonstrated in these two charming pictures, each displaying a pair of beautifully observed butterflies. Stitch and frame them as shown here or, alternatively, you might embroider all four on a single piece of fabric and frame them in a traditional glass case.

BUTTERFLIES

YOU WILL NEED

For either the *Gatekeeper and Tortoiseshell* or the
Painted lady and Peacock picture,
each set in a frame with a centre measuring
14cm × 9.5cm (5½ × 3½in):

*25cm × 20cm (10in × 8in) of antique white,
14-count Aida fabric
Stranded embroidery cotton in the colours given
in the appropriate panel*

*No24 tapestry needle
Picture frame, with an aperture as specified above
Firm card, to fit the frame
Lightweight synthetic batting, the same size
as the card
Strong thread, for mounting
Glue stick*

*NOTE: if you only wish to stitch one
of these pictures, you
will not require every colour
listed – check with the relevant chart;
one skein of each colour listed is
sufficient for both pictures.*

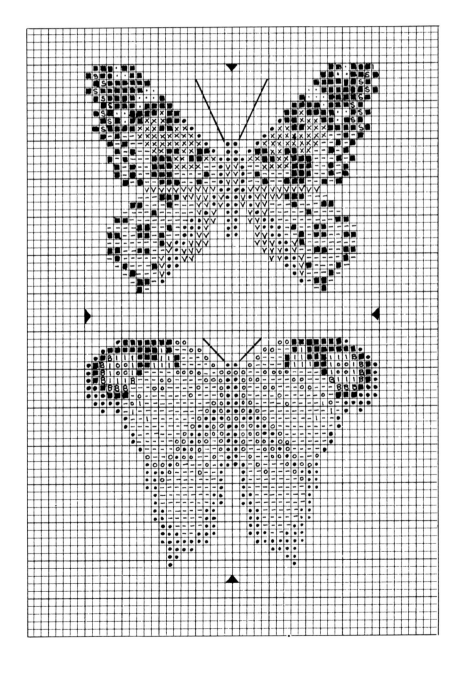

Top: Painted Lady
Bottom: Peacock

Top: Gatekeeper
Bottom: Tortoiseshell

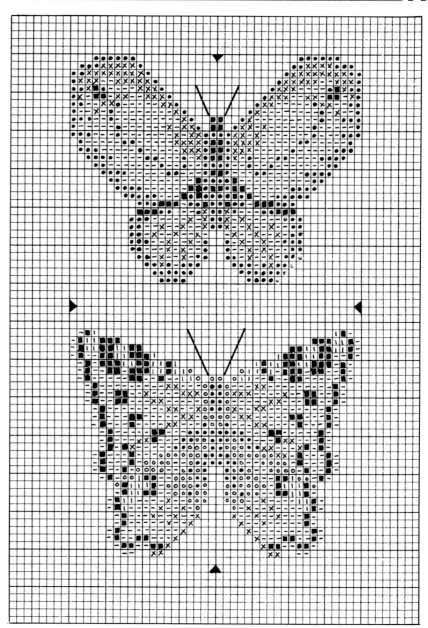

THE EMBROIDERY

Prepare the fabric as described on page 4; find the centre either by folding the fabric in half and then in half again, and lightly pressing the folded corner, or by marking the horizontal and vertical centre lines with basting stitches in a light-coloured thread. Mount the fabric in a frame (see page 5) and count out from the centre to start the design at an appropriate point.

Following the chart, complete all the cross stitching first, using two strands of thread in the needle. Finish with the antennae, again using two strands of thread. Be careful not to take dark threads across the back of the work in such a way that they show through on the right side.

MOUNTING AND FRAMING

Remove the finished embroidery from the frame and wash if necessary, then press lightly on the wrong side, using a steam iron. Spread glue evenly on one side of the mounting card, and lightly press the batting to the surface. Lace the embroidery over the padded surface (see page 6), using the basting stitches (if any) to check that the embroidery is centred over the card. Remove basting stitches, place the mounted embroidery in the frame, and assemble the frame according to the manufacturer's instructions.

BUTTERFLIES ▲	ANCHOR	DMC	MADEIRA
■ Black	403	310	Black
● Dark brown	905	3031	2003
O Rust	370	433	2008
v Light brown	375	420	2104
− Light orange	314	741	201
X Deep orange	316	740	203
I Lemon yellow	293	727	110
B Pale blue	128	775	1101
• White	1	Blanc	White
S Grey	399	318	1802

Note: embroider antennae in dark brown, using two strands of thread in the needle and making each antenna with one long straight stitch.

23

Wild Flower Cushion

Equally suitable for a living room or bedroom, this charming and delicate cushion will bring the beauty of wild flowers into your home even in the depths of winter.

WILD FLOWER
CUSHION

YOU WILL NEED

For the cushion cover, measuring
30cm (12in) square:

40cm (16in) square of pink, 14-count Aida fabric
40cm (16in) square of pink cotton fabric,
for the cover back
Stranded embroidery cotton in the colours
given in the panel
No26 tapestry needle
1.3m (1½yds) of green cord, for trimming
Matching pink and green sewing cotton
Cushion pad (for a plump effect, choose a cushion
pad slightly larger than the measurements of
the finished cover)

•

THE EMBROIDERY

Prepare the fabric as described on page 4; find the centre either by folding the fabric in half and then in half again, and lightly pressing the folded corner, or by marking the horizontal and vertical centre lines with basting stitches in a light-coloured thread. Mount the fabric in a frame (see page 5) and count out from the centre to start at an appropriate point.

Following the chart, complete all the cross stitching, using two strands of thread in the needle. Be careful not to take dark threads across the back of the work in such a way that they show through on the right side.

MAKING THE COVER

Remove the finished embroidery from the frame and wash if necessary, then press lightly on the wrong side, using a steam iron. Keeping the embroidery centred, trim the embroidery fabric to measure 32.5cm (13in) square. Place the embroidery and backing fabric with right sides together and machine stitch around the edges, taking a 12mm (½in) seam allowance and leaving a 25cm (10in) gap at one side edge.

Trim across the seam allowance at the corners, to remove excess fabric, and turn the cover right side out. Insert the cushion pad into the cover, fold in the remaining seam allowances and slipstitch the opening, leaving a small gap at one end for the cord

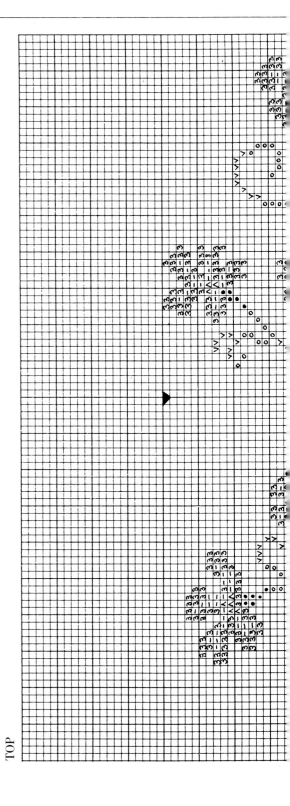

TOP

ends. Pin the cord trim around the edge of the cushion cover, tucking one end into the opening. Neatly slipstitch the cord in place, tucking the remaining end into the opening when you reach the starting point again, and stitching across the opening to seal it.

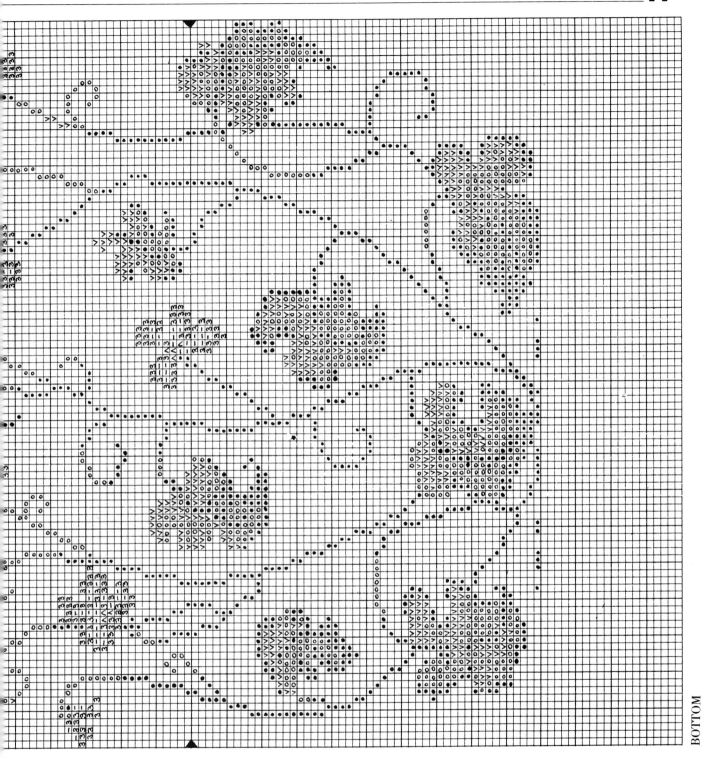

WILD FLOWER ▲ CUSHION		ANCHOR	DMC	MADEIRA
•	Light green	261	3363	1602
O	Medium green	262	3364	1603
V	Dark green	263	935	1505
−	Lilac	98	553	712
3	Purple	101	552	713
Λ	Yellow	306	725	113

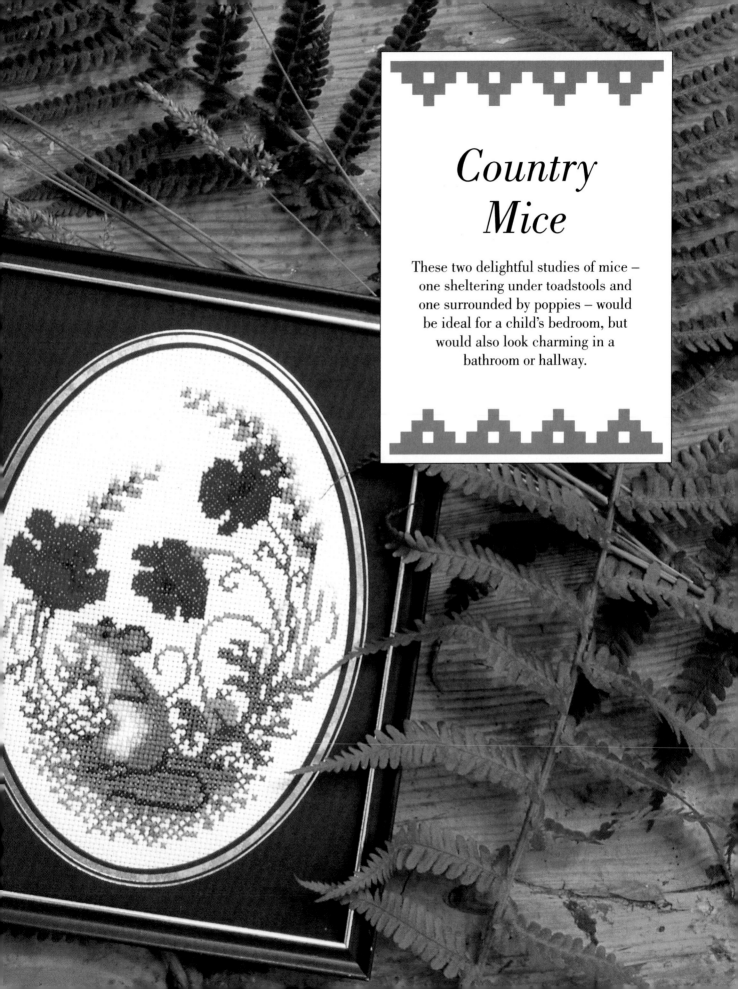

Country Mice

These two delightful studies of mice –
one sheltering under toadstools and
one surrounded by poppies – would
be ideal for a child's bedroom, but
would also look charming in a
bathroom or hallway.

COUNTRY MICE

YOU WILL NEED

For either the *Toadstool Mouse* or the *Poppy Mouse*
picture, each set in a frame measuring
23cm × 18cm (9in × 7in), with an oval cut-out
measuring 19cm × 14cm (7½ × 5½in):

*30cm × 27.5cm (12in × 11in) of white,
14-count Aida fabric
Stranded embroidery cotton in the colours
given in the panel*

*No24 tapestry needle
One small dark brown or black bead (optional)
Picture frame
Picture mount to fit the frame, with an oval aperture
as specified above
Firm card, to fit the frame
Lightweight synthetic batting, the same size
as the card
Strong thread, for mounting
Glue stick*

*NOTE: one skein of each colour listed is
sufficient for both pictures.*

Poppy Mouse ▶

THE EMBROIDERY

Prepare the fabric as described on page 4; find the centre either by folding the fabric in half and then in half again, and lightly pressing the folded corner, or by marking the horizontal and vertical centre lines with basting stitches in a light-coloured thread. Mount the fabric in a frame (see page 5) and count out from the centre to start at an appropriate point.

Following the chart, complete all the cross stitching first, using two strands of thread in the needle. Finish with the eye of the mouse, which is formed by one dark brown cross stitch. If you choose, you may add a small bead to the eye, which will bring it to life.

MOUNTING THE FRAMING

Remove the finished embroidery from the frame and wash if necessary, then press lightly on the wrong side, using a steam iron. Spread glue evenly on one side of the firm card, and lightly press the batting to the surface. Lace the embroidery over the padded surface (see page 6), using the basting stitches (if any) to check that the embroidery is centred over the card. Remove basting stitches, place the mounted embroidery in the frame, behind the oval mount, and assemble the frame according to the manufacturer's instructions.

COUNTRY MICE		ANCHOR	DMC	MADEIRA
•	White	2	Blanc	White
–	Cream	300	745	111
C	Light green	238	703	1307
O	Medium green	258	904	1413
●	Dark green	245	986	1405
2	Bright red	335	606	209
3	Medium red	19	817	212
4	Dark red	20	498	513
I	Beige	381	938	2005
H	Light brown	374	420	2104
■	Dark brown	380	839	1913

The Beauty of Trees

These cool, refreshing cards featuring four trees – elm, horse chestnut, cedar and fir – are suitable for many occasions. These simple yet strong images from nature would make a perfect keepsake to treasure for their lucky recipients.

THE BEAUTY OF TREES

YOU WILL NEED

For the *Elm, Horse Chestnut, Cedar or Fir*, each set
in a card with an oval aperture measuring
12.5cm × 9cm (5in × 3½in):

17.5cm × 12.5cm (7in × 5in) of white,
18-count Aida fabric
Stranded embroidery cotton in the colours given
in the appropriate panel
No26 tapestry needle
Card with an aperture as specified above
(for suppliers, see page 48)

NOTE: one skein of each colour listed is
sufficient for all four designs.

•

THE EMBROIDERY

Prepare the fabric as described on page 4; find the
centre either by folding the fabric in half and then in
half again, and lightly pressing the folded corner, or
by marking the horizontal and vertical centre lines
with basting stitches in a light-coloured thread.
Mount the fabric in a hoop (see page 4) and start the
embroidery at the centre of the design.

Following the chart, complete all the cross
stitching, using two strands of thread in the needle.

MOUNTING AND FRAMING

Remove the finished embroidery from the frame and
remove any basting stitches. Wash if necessary, then
press lightly on the wrong side, using a steam iron.
Trim the embroidery to measure about 12mm (½in)
larger all around than the size of the card window.
Position the embroidery behind the window; open
out the self-adhesive mount; fold the card, and press
firmly to secure it. Some cards require a dab of glue
to ensure a secure and neat finish.

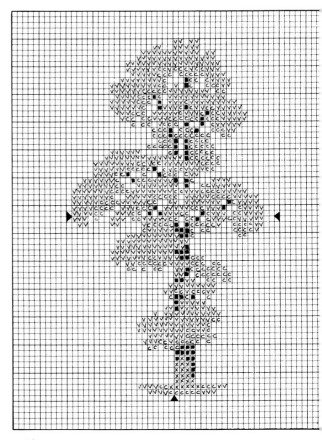

▲ Elm

TREES		ANCHOR	DMC	MADEIRA
v	Light yellow green	238	703	1307
C	Dark yellow green	258	904	1413
○	Medium green	243	988	1402
●	Dark green	245	986	1405
X	Light brown	358	433	2008
■	Dark brown	360	898	2006
•	White	1	Blanc	White

ELM ▲		ANCHOR	DMC	MADEIRA
v	Light yellow green	703	703	1307
C	Dark yellow green	258	904	1413
X	Light brown	358	433	2008
■	Dark brown	360	898	2006

HORSE CHESTNUT ▶		ANCHOR	DMC	MADEIRA
○	Medium green	243	988	1402
●	Dark green	245	986	1405
X	Light brown	358	433	2008
■	Dark brown	360	898	2006
•	White	1	Blanc	White

CEDAR ▶		ANCHOR	DMC	MADEIRA
v	Light yellow green	238	703	1307
C	Dark yellow green	258	904	1413
X	Light brown	358	433	2008
■	Dark brown	360	898	2006

FIR ▶		ANCHOR	DMC	MADEIRA
●	Dark green	245	986	1405
X	Light brown	358	433	2008
■	Dark brown	360	898	2006

► Cedar

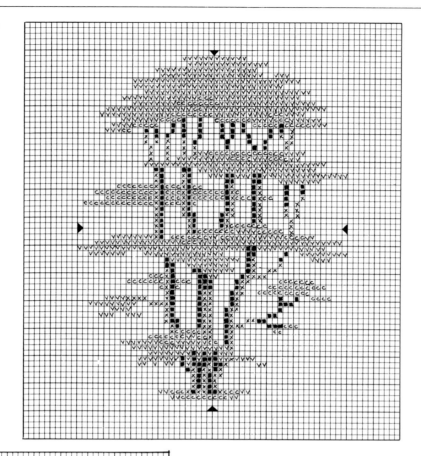

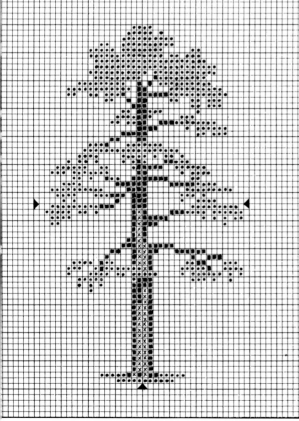

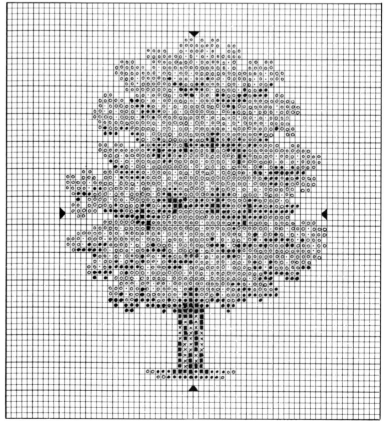

▲ Horse Chestnut

Down on the Farm

The countryside is not only very beautiful, but also extremely bountiful. This matching pair of pictures, showing ploughing and the fruit harvest, celebrate the work of the country farmer.

DOWN ON THE FARM

YOU WILL NEED

For either the *Ploughing* or the *Apple Picking* picture, each set in a frame with a centre measuring 17.5cm × 15cm (7in × 6in):

30cm × 27.5cm (12in × 11in) of white, 14-count Aida fabric
Stranded embroidery cotton in the colours given in the panel
No24 tapestry needle
Picture frame, as specified above
Firm card, to fit the frame

Lightweight synthetic batting, the same size as the card
Strong thread, for mounting
Glue stick

NOTE: one skein of each colour listed is sufficient for both pictures.

●

THE EMBROIDERY

Prepare the fabric as described on page 4; find the centre either by folding the fabric in half and then in half again, and lightly pressing the folded corner, or by marking the horizontal and vertical centre lines with basting stitches in a light-coloured thread.

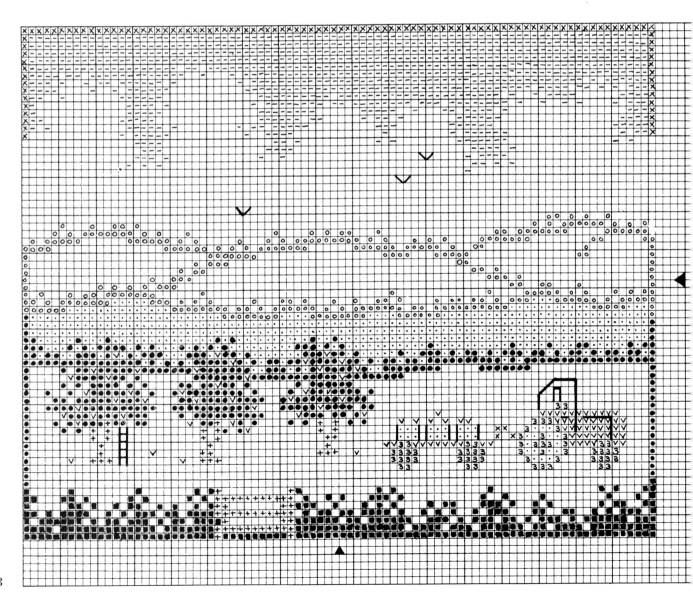

Mount the fabric in a hoop (see page 4) and start the embroidery at the centre of the design.

Following the chart, complete all the cross stitching, using two strands of thread in the needle. Finish with the backstitched details, again using two strands of thread in the needle. Be careful not to take dark threads across the back of the work in such a way that they show through on to the right side of the embroidery.

MOUNTING AND FRAMING

Remove the finished embroidery from the frame and wash if necessary, then press lightly on the wrong side, using a steam iron. Spread glue evenly on one side of the firm card, and lightly press the batting to the surface. Lace the embroidery over the padded surface (see page 6), using the basting stitches (if any) to check that the embroidery is centred over the card. Remove basting stitches, place the mounted embroidery in the frame, and assemble the frame according to the manufacturer's instructions.

DOWN ON THE FARM ▼		ANCHOR	DMC	MADEIRA
■	Dark green	245	986	1405
●	Medium green	243	988	1402
○	Light green	241	955	1210
•	Yellow	293	727	110
V	Red	13	349	212
3	Navy blue	127	939	1009
X	Medium blue	161	3760	1012
−	Pale blue	160	813	1002
+	Brown	352	300	2304

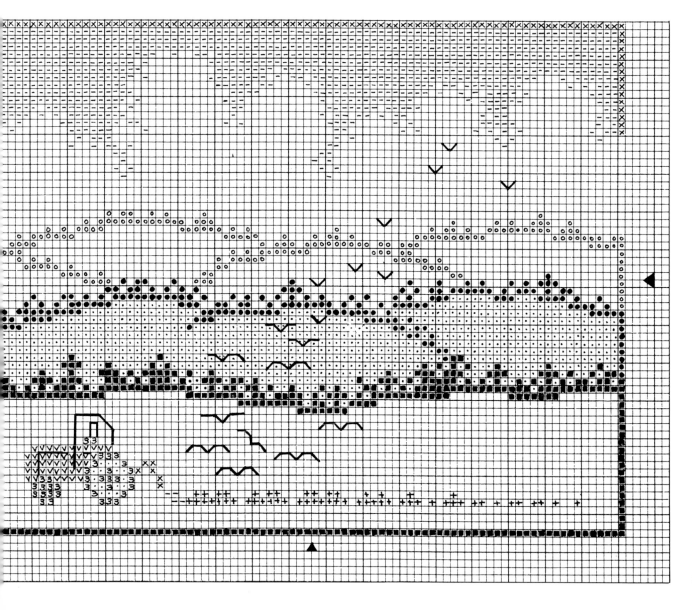

Daisy Patch Tablecloth

A fresh sprinkling of daisies lies in a diagonal pattern across this charming tablecloth, which would be ideal for lunch or tea on the lawn on a summer's day. If you choose, you might embroider the daisy motifs on a matching set of napkins.

DAISY PATCH TABLECLOTH

YOU WILL NEED

For the tablecloth, measuring
approximately 162cm (64in) square:

*1.75m (2yds) of Zweigart Favourite, 2215
(for suppliers, see page 48)
6m (6²⁄₃yds) of lace trim,
approximately 12mm (¹⁄₂in) deep
Stranded embroidery cotton in the colours given in
the panel; you will require one skein of orange and
three skeins of each of the other colours listed
No24 tapestry needle*

●

THE EMBROIDERY

Trim the cloth to make it a square, then either
overlock the edges by machine and turn and stitch a
4cm (1¹⁄₂in) hem or make a 12mm (¹⁄₂in) fold and
then a 2.5cm (1in) fold and handsew the hem. Pin
and stitch the lace trim in position along the folded
edge.

As can be seen in the diagram, the pattern runs
diagonally across the cloth, diagonal rows of daisy
patches, one to each Aida circle, alternating with
diagonal rows of single daisies. In order that the
cloth looks the same from the opposite sides, the
motifs are alternately stitched facing the right way
up, and then flipped vertically in the next circle to
face upside down.

It is important to use a hoop for this project (see
page 4), as the weave of the fabric is loose and the
stitching would otherwise deform the Aida circles.
Never leave your work in the hoop when you are not
stitching, as this can leave marks on the cloth.

Use three strands of thread in the needle for both
the cross stitching and the backstitched flower
stalks. Be careful not to take dark threads across the
back of the work in such a way that they show
through on the right side. It is also important to
ensure that threads are fastened securely, as the
tablecloth will need to withstand the rigours of
constant use and washing.

NAPKINS

If you wish to make a set of table napkins to match
your cloth, you can either use the same fabric,
allowing approximately a 45cm (17in) square of

fabric for each napkin, or purchase ready-prepared
napkins from the suppliers listed on page 48.

Choose your motif (you might decide to set the
single flower at one corner and the patch of daisies
at the opposite corner of each napkin). Work out how
far from the edge you wish to set each motif, then
count up an even number of threads from each side
of the corner and baste guidelines along each edge,
crossing at the corner, to help to ensure that the
motif is correctly positioned.

THE DAISY PATCH ▶	ANCHOR	DMC	MADEIRA
○ Light blue	131	798	911
● Dark blue	132	797	912
v Light green	243	988	1402
∧ Dark green	245	986	1405
— Orange	314	741	201

Note: bks flower stalks in dark green.

Positioning the
motifs

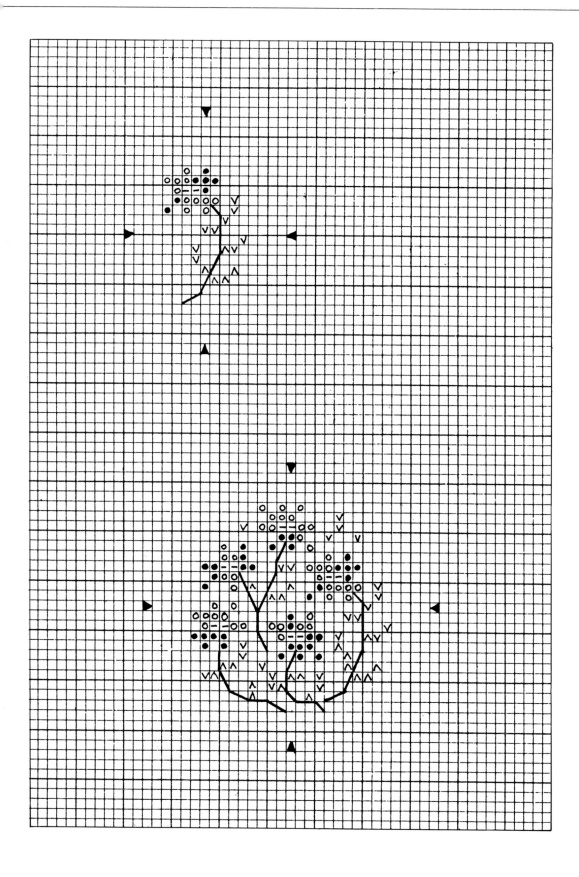

Wildlife
Studies

Make them as five separate cards to
delight your family and friends, or
combine them into a single charming
picture – whichever you choose, this
set of wildlife studies will prove
enjoyable to stitch. The individual
designs are relatively simple and
could prove a pleasant exercise for
a child learning embroidery.

WILDLIFE STUDIES

YOU WILL NEED

For the picture, set in a frame with a centre measuring 22.5cm × 17.5cm (9in × 7in):

35cm × 30cm (14in × 12in) of antique white, 14-count Aida fabric
Stranded embroidery cotton in the colours given in the panel
No26 tapestry needle
Picture frame, as specified above
Firm card, to fit the frame
Lightweight synthetic batting, the same size as the card
Strong thread, for mounting
Glue stick

For each card:

15cm × 12.5cm (6in × 5in) of antique white, 14-count Aida fabric
Stranded embroidery cotton in the colours given in the panel
No26 tapestry needle
Card with an aperture measuring 10cm × 7.5cm (4in × 3in), designed for embroidery (for suppliers, see page 48)

•

THE EMBROIDERY

Prepare the fabric as described on page 4; find the centre either by folding the fabric in half and then in half again, and lightly pressing the folded corner, or by marking the horizontal and vertical centre lines with basting stitches in a light-coloured thread. If you are making the picture, mount the fabric in a frame (see page 5); individual designs can be stitched without a frame.

Count out from the centre to start at an appropriate point. Following the chart, complete the cross stitching first, using two strands of thread in the needle. Finish with the backstitched details, again using two strands of thread in the needle. Be careful not to take dark threads across the back of the work in such a way that they show through on to the right side of the embroidery. Remove the finished embroidery from the frame, if used, and wash if necessary, then press lightly on the wrong side, using a steam iron.

MOUNTING THE PICTURE

Spread glue evenly on one side of the firm card, and lightly press the batting to the surface. Lace the embroidery over the padded surface (see page 6), using the basting stitches (if any) to check that the embroidery is centred over the card. Remove basting stitches, place the mounted embroidery in the frame, and assemble the frame according to the manufacturer's instructions.

THE CARDS

For each card, trim the embroidery to measure about 12mm (½in) larger all around than the size of the card window. Remove basting stitches. Position the embroidery behind the window; open out the self-adhesive mount; fold the card, and press firmly to secure it. Some cards require a dab of glue to ensure a secure and neat finish.

WILDLIFE STUDIES ▶	ANCHOR	DMC	MADEIRA
• White	1	Blanc	White
− Silver grey	397	453	1807
I Medium grey	399	318	1802
X Dark grey	400	317	1714
■ Black	403	310	Black
C Light warm brown	369	435	2010
O Medium warm brown	370	433	2008
+ Dark warm brown	371	739	2303
● Dark brown	905	3781	2106
V Light grass green	226	702	1306
∧ Medium grass green	228	700	1304

Note: bks ears of squirrel, badger, rabbit and pole cat in black, and badger's eye in white.

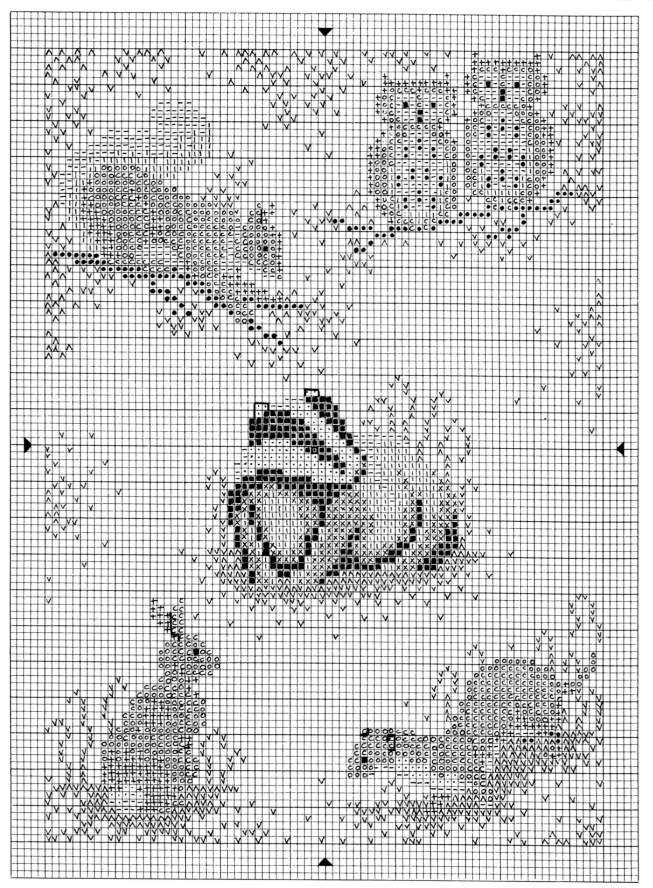

ACKNOWLEDGEMENTS

My grateful thanks go to my family and friends for their invaluable help. I would like to thank all those who helped to stitch the projects, in particular, Cynthia Sherwood, Ann Midwood, Sylvia Read and my daughter Elizabeth Marsh.

Thanks are also due to Coats Patons Crafts for supplying most of the materials and threads used in this book and to Willow Fabrics for the table linen.

SUPPLIERS

Fabric for the daisy patch tablecloth on page 40 was obtained from:

Willow Fabrics
27, Willow Green
Knutsford, WA16 6AX
Telephone: 0565 621098

The following mail order company is also useful as a supply source for cross stitch items including blank embroidery cards, picture frames and linens:

Framecraft Miniatures Limited
372/376 Summer Lane
Hockley
Birmingham, B19 3QA
England
Telephone: 021 212 0551

Addresses for Framecraft stockists worldwide
Ireland Needlecraft Pty Ltd
2-4 Keppel Drive
Hallam, Victoria 3803
Australia

Danish Art Needlework
PO Box 442, Lethbridge
Alberta T1J 3Z1
Canada
Sanyei Imports
PO Box 5, Hashima Shi
Gifu 501-62
Japan

The Embroidery Shop
286 Queen Street
Masterton
New Zealand

Anne Brinkley Designs Inc.
246 Walnut Street
Newton
Mass. 02160
USA

S A Threads and Cottons Ltd.
43 Somerset Road
Cape Town
South Africa

For information on your nearest stockist of embroidery cotton, contact the following:

DMC
(also distributors of Zweigart fabrics)

UK
DMC Creative World Limited
62 Pullman Road
Wigston
Leicester, LE8 2DY
Telephone: 0533 811040

USA
The DMC Corporation
Port Kearney Bld.
10 South Kearney
N.J. 07032-0650
Telephone: 201 589 0606

AUSTRALIA
DMC Needlecraft Pty
P.O. Box 317
Earlswood 2206
NSW 2204
Telephone: 02599 3088

COATS AND ANCHOR
Coats Paton Crafts
McMullen Road
Darlington
Co. Durham DL1 1YQ
Telephone: 0325 381010

USA
Coats & Clark
P.O. Box 27067
Dept CO1
Greenville
SC 29616
Telephone: 803 234 0103

AUSTRALIA
Coats Patons Crafts
Thistle Street
Launceston
Tasmania 7250
Telephone: 00344 4222

MADEIRA
UK
Madeira Threads (UK) Limited
Thirsk Industrial Park
York Road, Thirsk
N. Yorkshire, YO7 3BX
Telephone: 0845 524880

USA
Madeira Marketing Limited
600 East 9th Street
Michigan City
IN 46360
Telephone: 219 873 1000

AUSTRALIA
Penguin Threads Pty Limited
25-27 Izett Street
Prahran
Victoria 3181
Telephone: 03529 4400